How to Train and Understand A Irish Setter Puppy or Dog with Good Behavior

How to Train and Understand A Irish Setter Puppy or Dog with Good Behavior

Copyright © 2011 by Vince Stead

ISBN: 978-1460978474

www.vincestead.com

1. THE CHARACTERISTICS OF AN IRISH SETTER PUPPY AND DOG

"The Irish Setter, also known as the Red Setter sometimes, is a very remarkable puppy and dog. They make excellent bird dogs for hunting, and they make excellent pets as family members."

"The Irish Setter is one of the best sporting and hunting dogs. They coat is the color of mahogany, chestnut or red, and their coat of hair is long and shiny. You must make sure you brush your Irish Setter on a regular basis, to keep snarls and matts out of it."

"The Irish Setter is a high energy dog, and needs lots of exercise and attention. If you just keep your dog in the back yard, and don't do much with him or her, they will get destructive. They need agility training for fun, obedience training, and plenty of exercise to keep them entertained."

"The Irish Setter comes from Ireland, and they were breed to be bird hunting dogs. An Irish Setter can smell the bird or game from far distances. The dog would point, or stand at a stance where it looks like he or she is pointing. They will flush out the birds and game, and they will swim out and retrieve the game and bring it back, when trained for it properly."

"Irish Setters are great with kids and other pets as long as they have been socialized at a young age with them. The only thing you might be concerned with, for a dog that has not been socialized correctly, would be small pets, since the Irish Setter has the natural instinct of looking for birds, so it is vital that your dog be introduced to small animals at an early age."

"The average size for an Irish Setter is roughly 50 to 70 pounds, with the males being larger, and weighing the most. Irish Setters have been used as animals that help kids read books, where the dog will sit in front of the child, and the child will read to the Irish Setter, to get the child used to reading in front of someone. They are also used in hospitals as therapy dogs."

"Irish Setters are fun loving dog, who make excellent family members. They do not make that good of a guard dog, as being aggressive is not really in their nature, but a bark still might scare a burglar away, but don't buy one as a guard dog, because they just might lick the burglar."

"Irish Setters have a life expectancy of about 12 to 15 years. Your Irish Setter really has a job to do. They love to be out in the open, and love the water and hunting. You really need to make sure your Irish Setter is entertained, and exercised on a regular basis."

"In the 1940's, the Irish Setter was slowly dwindling in numbers. The magazines "Field and Stream" and "Sports Afield" took charge, and ran articles about increasing the dog breed, and making a comeback, which has worked."

"Some famous Irish Setters you may know include: Alex, the dog from the Stroh's beer commercials. Big Red, from the movies, and presidents Harry Truman and Richard Nixon both owned Irish Setters. The well-known Dog Whisper, Cesar Millan's first dog was an Irish Setter."

2. WHY AN IRISH SETTER IS A GOOD CHOICE FOR FAMILIES

"Irish Setters are such a fun loving beautiful dog! Irish Setters are perfect family dogs, as they love companionship, being with families, being with people in general. Irish Setters are lovable, smart, easy to train, good temperament, great addition to any family or household usually."

"Irish setters make very good watch dogs but any dog in the home is more likely to scare away a burglar, than no dog at all. They are great with children, when socialized correctly when they are young"

"Irish Setters are very special dogs. The average size Irish Setter will be anywhere from 120 to 200 pounds, males usually weighing the most. They need plenty of love and exercise, as they are a large breed dog."

3. How to Stop Your Irish Setter From Jumping Up On People

"It is your dog's way of getting your attention, and the best way her or she knows, is jumping up on you when they see you, and want to greet you, and get some attention from you."

"This is almost always cute when your Irish Setter is a puppy, but when he or she gets bigger, that would be a big dog you have jumping up! You need to teach your puppy not to jump up and get excited when they see you."

"Some of the best ways to teach your Irish Setter not to jump up on people, and you don't want guests and family members avoiding your big giant dog that jumps up on people, now do you!"

"The best way to curb this is to not be excited when you see your dog, and don't make eye contact. When your dog goes to jump up on you, turn your body so he or she slides down. Keep doing this, and don't talk to the dog, just use your body language, and keep turning to the side, until your dog finally settles down, and then when he or she is standing calm, give them praise for being calm."

"Your Irish Setter should learn to be calmer, and they will get the praise they desire, much sooner. Make sure you have all the other family members on board, if one person lets the dog jump up, he or she will be confused, so get the whole family into the training program!"

"Your puppy more dog will not grasp this right away, but with proper training, and repetitive training, your dog will become a much better family member!"

4. What You Should Know About Puppy Teeth

"There is no doubt about it; puppies are going to chew on things! Dogs will have 28 baby teeth, and 42 permanent teeth. When a puppy is roughly, 2 to 3 weeks old, their baby teeth start to come in. All their baby teeth should be in place by roughly 8 weeks of age."

"The puppies' new teeth are very tiny and sharp, and will hurt your fingers when they get a hold of them. Most mothers will start to wean their babies at 5 to 6 weeks old."

"Your puppies baby teeth will start to come out around 8 to 12 weeks of age. By roughly 8 months old, your dog's permanent teeth should all be in. You should make sure that all baby teeth are out, so that a tooth does not get left in, and another one come in and crowd the space, and give your dog pain. You would need to visit the vet if you see this happening."

"Your puppy is going to want to chew on something, just like a real baby, their teeth are coming in, and they want to relieve some for the pain, and it is good for them to chew, to help the teeth come thru. You would want to get some appropriate chew items to help them."

"You could start to train your dog to have their teeth brushed. You can pick up doggie tooth supplies at your local pet store usually, and get down and dirty, and brush your doggies' teeth. Rawhide chews are an excellent source of good tooth hygiene, as they are good for your dog's teeth, and can help take off build up plaque, and dogs usually love it also!"

"A lot of puppies and dogs end up getting human food, usually from the weakest link in the family. If your dog is under the table, they usually will go to the person they think will mostly likely give them some food scraps. If you do, just remember, chocolate and some nuts can kill your dog never give chocolate. Raisins can be just as deadly for your dog, do not give, they can shut down your dog's kidneys, so be very careful of these products and your puppy or dog."

5. SOME HELPFUL TIPS FOR RAISING YOUR IRISH SETTER PUPPY

"Before you bring your Irish Setter puppy home, you might want to get things ready for him or her. Some of the things you might want to get would include:"

"Some dog crates, one or two for the house, and one for the car. You would want to get some fencing for the back yard, and as you know, Irish Setter are going to be really big dogs when they grow up! You might as well get the heaviest duty dog gear you can buy, it will be worth it!"

"You would want to get your home and yard ready just like you would for a new baby almost. You would want to puppy proof your home, nothing that would hurt the puppy should be out, and all cabinets should be locked."

"For outside the house, all pools and hot tubs should be fenced in, and all gates should be locked and double checked. A Irish Setter can really put a lot of weight into something, if you think they might get out, they probably can, so make it even tougher, it's a Irish Setter!"

"Collars and leashes, you would actually need several, for training purposes. A short one for training and a long one for walks you go on. You should not leave a collar on a puppy while unsupervised, it could get caught and choke the puppy."

"A collar should be used only when training. They are common on most every dog, just make sure you have a good fitting one, and watch your puppy, to make sure he or she does not get it caught, a collar should not be left on, but dog owners do it all the time it seems, so just be extra careful."

"You should never have to yell or scream, or get carried away when trying to train your Irish Setter. If you feel he or she is not moving forward, take a break, and try it again in a bit. Make sure you are not the one who is trying too hard. To puppy will learn the commands, over time, no puppy gets it all right the first time, there will be mistakes, but in the long run, you will have a much better trained dog. One you and your family can live with for many years to come!"

"While your puppy is still young, you should enroll yourself and your new puppy in as many dog obedient classes that you think you could handle. This will be the best experience for both you and your puppy, and you both will bond much better together, and get the most out of it. For the long haul, it is totally worth it!"

"Hopefully your puppy has already seen the vet before you even brought him home, just for a checkup at least. You should at this time, find a reputable vet in your area, and set your new puppy up for regular visits and exams all puppies and dogs need to have on a regular basis."

"The first day you bring you new puppy home, try to make it when you have plenty of time off of work or school, so that the puppy is not immediate left alone, and insecure. It is best to spend plenty of time with the new puppy, especially the first couple of days."

"If you can take a sock or towel with you, and let the mother and any other siblings roll around on it, it would be a good comfort blanket to help your new puppy adjust in his new home."

"Your puppy might whine, whimper and cry the first couple of nights, this is natural really. It will go away eventually, as this is how its mother raises the baby. It whines when it cries for its mother, when it wants to eat, and is crying out for attention."

"That is where the towel or sock with the mothers scent rubbed on it, comes in handy to put inside the crate. You would also want some good solid stainless steel bowls for food and water. You should check with your vet on a proper food and feeding time, usually twice daily, at the same times, but some vets recommend different diets for your Irish Setter, so check with your vet first."

"Teach your new Irish Setter puppy to be a part of the family. Irish Setter dogs like to be included with the family, they are not that happy if just left in the back yard, they like to be included with the family, so keep that in mind and have fun with your new Irish Setter puppy!"

"You can teach your new puppy to go to the bathroom outside. You need to take your new puppy outside several times a day. A puppy cannot tell you when they have to go pee or poop they just go. It is your responsibility to know to take the puppy outside, since they will have to go to the bathroom several times each day."

"When you take your new puppy outside, teach them to eliminate in a certain spot, and then give them a treat and praise. Continue to do this, each time you take them outside, tell them to go "potty" and wait for them to go. As soon as they are done, reward them with praise and a treat, and take them back inside."

"When take your puppy outside to go to the bathroom, when you take him or her out, just stand still, and let the dog do their business. When they are finally doing their business, while they are doing it, just stand there, and say, "Good Potty" "Good Baby" and talk sweet to them, until they are done."

"When they are done, give them praise and a treat. Continue doing this until you only use praise, and the dog will learn to go outside, and do his or her businesses quickly, and then back inside."

"Under no circumstances should you ever leave your new puppy unsupervised. If you have to do something, he or she should be in their crate, safe and sound."

6. How to Crate Train Your Irish Setter

"If you were a new Irish Setter puppy, wouldn't you want your new home to be warm, comfortable, secure and inviting? Sure you would, and your new Irish Setter puppy, or even a full grown older dog, loves a nice secure home to sleep in!"

"You want your Irish Setter puppy or dog to have a secure place to rest and go to, when you want them to be in a secure place, while you're away."

"To begin with a new puppy, you would want to have a good size crate, one they can stand up and lie down in, and turn around comfortably, but not to big either."

"You would want to leave the door open in the beginning, and just get your Irish Setter used to the crate. You would put a treat at the opening of the crate, and let your Irish Setter go and eat it. You would continue until you are putting the treats in the back of the crate, and your Irish Setter feels comfortable going inside."

"You want them to get used to getting a treat for going inside, and then later turn it into praise. This will be their home. You would put their food and water inside, and with training, it will become their own little den, a place they like to sleep."

"After you have your Irish Setter going inside, it is time to shut the door jut for a very short period of time, 1 to 2 minutes, and you would give your Irish Setter a treat while inside, and praise, then open the door back up. You never want to use the crate as punishment, don't put them in the crate when they have been bad, they will associate that with being put in the crate, you want them to feel secure in their spot."

"Put their crate out of the way, but not totally out of the way, somewhere in a room the family shares, but in his or her own little corner, makes it a nice home for them."

"If you are going to be gone, and have to leave your Irish Setter in his crate for a long period of time, try to get them their favorite toys, or a toy with a snack inside, that takes time to get out. They are occupied for a while, because you want them to associate going into their crate, as a fun place to go."

7. WHEN YOUR IRISH SETTER MAKES POTTY MISTAKES

"Too many dogs have been abandoned at animal shelters, just for the sole purpose of the dog making potty mistakes in the wrong places, and not being properly trained."

"Irish setters sometimes might go potty in response to fear, excitement, separation anxiety, marking territory, and sometimes medical problems. It is best to start with your vet about any medical problems, before you move forward. Some dogs may have a urinary infection, and spayed females may have some small leaking at times where they lie down or sleep."

"One of the most common symptoms is separation anxiety. If the dog has gone thru some new changes, or there has been a change in the household, it could be affecting your Irish Setter."

"Another problem might be submissive urination, which occurs when your dog first sees you when you come home, uncontrollable urinating and submissive behavior, like rolling on his or her back."

"One way to help remedy this is to immediately take your Irish Setter outside right when you get home, and try to stay calm and low beat when just greeting your dog, to help him or her get less excited."

"Some dogs will perform a marking behavior by lifting their hind leg and urinating. This is most common in unneutered male dogs that have not been neutered. If a male dog is neutered around 6 months of age, this will usually, cure this behavior. A male dog should be neutered if he is not intended for breeding, or there is a medical reason while your Irish Setter should not be neutered."

"If you see your Irish Setter getting ready to go potty, immediately clap your hands together, or use another device to get their attention, and immediately take them outside."

"A dog is not considered housebroken until he or she has not had an accident for around 45 days in a row. You can easily train your young Irish Setter to go outside; when you notice that he or she is sniffing around as if they want to go. After they just ate, had a bath, just woke up and just your gut instinct that your Irish Setter might go potty inside."

"If you need to be gone from your Irish Setter for an extended period of time, you should keep him or her in a crate or cage. Make sure you do not give them an oversize crate or cage, or they will use that space to go potty."

"If you need to train an adult Irish Setter, do it just like you would a puppy! Give them the right guidance, and train them just as if you would a puppy. An adult dog needs to urinate roughly 3 to 4 times a day, and defecate once or twice daily."

"When your puppy or adult Irish Setter does a bad thing inside, in a firm and stern voice, say "bad dog", and then take then outside where you would like them to go, and tell them "good dog." Give praise when your Irish Setter goes outside."

"To potty train a puppy or adult dog, you must lay down newspapers, and bring the puppy to the newspapers, and say "good dog" at that spot. When you catch your puppy starting to go, get them if you still can, and tell them "bad dog", and then put them on the newspaper, and tell them "good dog", and after they go, give them praise."

"You would start out with a wide section of newspapers on the floor in the beginning, and then slowly you can decrease the size to a manageable spot. Give your Irish Setter a little time to use to this, they will learn to go on the newspapers, when they get praise, and get a stern voice when they go in the wrong spot, they would rather have praise, and will learn!"

8. Some Items You Should Never Let Your Puppy or Dog Eat

"Some items you should never let a puppy or dog eat, because it can harm or kill them, so you should be aware of them. I'm sure most people already know you should never give a puppy or dog chocolate, not even a little piece. Chocolate usually has caffeine in it, and even just a small amount, could kill a puppy or dog, or put them into convulsions."

"Just like people, some big guys can eat 15 hot dogs, and 5 bottles of beer, and the next guy can't even eat 1 hot dog, and would never finish a bottle of beer, that is just an example really. A puppy or dog is the same way; no two dogs are going to be alike. Some dogs might be fine eating broccoli, and other dogs might bite the bullet from it, so it's just nice to know what kinds of foods could hurt your dog, and this list could change at any time really."

"Some items you would not want to give your dog might include: raisins and grapes, macadamia nuts, walnuts, cooked bones (raw bones are good, cooked bones splinter and can hurt your dog much easier that raw soft fresh bones.) You would not give avocado, onions, garlic, mushrooms, broccoli, tea or coffee, white bread, white potatoes, white rice, peppers, raw spinach and probably some other things your vet might have on a list for your dog."

"Granted, some dogs might have been eating some of these products for years, but all young children need to be taught, that giving even the smallest amount of chocolate to a puppy or dog, can be deadly, even the candy bar wrappers on the ground, a dog might try to lick it up."

"Teach children that candy has no place in a dog's life. Some dogs cannot digest broccoli for example very well, and other dogs might be just fine, but it is better to find alternative foods, since the world has so many kinds."

"The best food of all is food you make yourself, since you can actually see the real ingredients going into it. Some super market dog foods are so full of corn and soybeans, you wonder if your dog gets any nutrition from it, unless he or she eats the whole bag, and that could be the case. If you learn the fix your dog healthy food at home, and leave out the stuff that might hurt or kill him or her, you would be doing your dog a big favor!"

9. MAKE IT EASIER AND HEALTHIER FOR FEEDING YOUR IRISH SETTER

"You can make is much easier on your Irish Setter when it comes to eating. Some dogs you can leave their food out for them, and they do not over eat. Other dogs may over eat until they get bloat, or they gobble it down super-fast, and have gas problems and more serious problems."

"To find out how much your dog should be eating, you should check with your vet. You could also measure your dog's food, and then feed him or her twice a day. If they eat the whole bowl, give them more next time, if they don't eat it all, give them less each time. You could measure it, and then come up with the right amount for your dog for each meal."

"For dogs that gobble down their food so fast, the pet supply places, sell dog bowls that have inserts in the bowl, so the dog would have to slow down to eat. You would never want to give your dog just one meal a day. You should feed them twice a day, and at the same time each day, so they can count on their schedule, just like people seem to love, breakfast, lunch and dinner!"

"For large size dogs, it is harder on them and their joints when they have to bend over, to get their head down to the ground, to get a drink of water, and that is bad for their joints, especially if they are young still. Some pet supply stores sell water and food bowls, that go in a stand and make it higher off the ground, and that makes it easier for your puppy or dog to swallow, as their body is more parallel to the ground while eating."

"Raised water and eating bowl, will make your dog more comfortable when eating, and it's especially great if they have muscle or joint problems, and you won't your dog to have a happy and healthy life."

"Just like people, so dogs don't drink enough water sometimes. If you can get your dog to drink more water, it will be much better and healthier for them. You can get one of the bowls from the pet supply store, that gives a continuous supply of cool water, and your dog might enjoy it even more!"

10. When Your Irish Setter Has Separation Anxiety, and How to Deal With It

"Separation anxiety can happen in any dog, at any age, and for any reason. Doctors are not very sure why this happens, but they agree that is happens more in dogs that were not properly nurtured as puppies, had new moves, or a new schedule. The dog might be moved around as a puppy, and these things can make a dog have separation anxiety."

"Some of the things a dog might do could be excessive, howling, barking, whining, pacing, chewing, scratching, digging, urinating and defecating. As the time goes on, the systems become worse; the dogs might break his teeth, rip his or her nails, and injure themselves. It seems to happen in pets, which did not have much socializing as puppies."

"One good way to teach your Irish Setter something good is to find a quiet place for just you and the dog, and get them to relax by you. When you have them relaxed, give them a treat. You can do this and slowly back away, and put more distance in between you and the dog, slowly separating the two of you."

"Another good technique, is be misleading your dog. They might be accustomed to your car keys shaking, meaning you are leaving, or you putting on your jacket, or other signs your dog might read, that lets them know you are leaving."

"Try picking up your car keys several times a day, and not leave. Put your jacket on, and take it back off, several times a day. Try to break up your dog's regular routine pattern, which you might not even think about. Your dog might already have a routine, that you subconsciously, don't even realize it."

"When you come home, pretend that you don't even notice the dog, until she or he has calmed down, and then when they have relaxed, give them a treat or praise."

"Another way is to give your dog some excitement. Could you imagine being cooped up all day long, while your owner is out working, and you have to play with the same old toy, day in and day out? If you turn the lights on 30 minutes early, or give your Irish Setter a new toy, which a secret treat inside, that will keep them occupied, and spice up their day, if you were a pet, would you not want to be treated that way?"

"Remember, young dogs still have lots of energy. If you come home, and find your favorite chair in threads, you might want to consider increasing your younger dogs exercise pattern, they should be exercised twice a day, from 30 to 45 minutes each time."

"You could teach them commands, tech them to play fetch, and other good times. Your Irish Setter needs plenty of exercise to feel like a dog. Most dogs were breed for a certain job, a herder, a Shepard, a hunting dog, and more. A dog had these instincts in their blood; you need to make sure they get plenty of exercise."

11. WHEN YOUR IRISH SETTER IS AFRAID OF LOUD NOISES

"If your Irish Setter has a fear of loud noises, gun shots, fireworks, thunderstorms, and other loud noises, is a very common among dogs. If he or she is displaying signs, like shaking, trembling, hiding, trying to run away, barking, urinating or uncontrollable pooping, these could be some of the signs."

"You can sometimes treat this with behavior modifications, general change of environment, and even prescription medicines."

"One of the best ways to make the dog better, is to change his or her own living environment around. You should increase the dogs daily exercise program, to make him physically more drained."

"Give your pet his or her own space. Pets love to feel secure and protected. Try to make the a crate or sleeping area, that give them comfort, and has some walls up around them, so they don't feel like that have to worry about things coming at them, from all directions. Dogs usually like to find nice places to relax and sleep, like under chairs, tables, places where they feel safe, they can sleep, and still keep one eye open, to make sure they stay out of harm's way."

"Give your Irish Setter a more noise friendly atmosphere. You could turn on a radio, or run a fan or other mechanical noisemaker that is peace full and continuous. This is good if the dog can hear noise outside, like kids yelling and playing, other dogs barking; construction going on, it helps tone down the noise, with other continuous noise, to calm the dog."

"Don't overly give your dog extra added attention, like petting him or her longer, they might interrupt that as a good reward for acting bad, just treat your dog normally."

"One fun way to try and teach your dog not to be afraid, is to give him or her their favorite treat or snack, each time the load noise is going to come. If it is a thunderstorm, each time the loud bang comes, give your dog a treat, they will look forward to more thunderstorms!"

"If you want to train your dog not to be afraid, you can obtain CD's or downloads from the internet, of thunderstorms, fireworks, gun shots, etc....and begin by letting your dog listen to these sounds, at low volume. You will gradually increase the volume over time, and give your dog a treat when she does not freak out to the sound, and slowly increase the volume each training session, then slowly do less and less training, until your Irish Setter does not have any more fear of the loud noises."

"If this does not suit you, there are medicines available from your veterinarian, that you can give to your dog, before a storm or load noises, to calm him or her, the old fashioned way, with prescription drugs."

"You should be able to find noises on line very easily, with all the major search engines, just type in thunderstorm sounds, and you will be on your way!"

12. How to Build A Whelping Box for an Irish Setter or Any Other Breed of Dog

"How to build a whelping box for your Irish Setter, or any other size dog for that matter. You can determine what size whelping box you need, by making sure your dog had plenty of room to walk around the whelping box. The purpose of the whelping box is to make sure that the mother does not get one of the puppies lodged between her and the box, and squeezes them to death."

"Irish Setter's, or any other large size dog, can easily smoother their young, if they get laid on. I think the best way to make a nice whelping box for a Irish Setter is to take a full sheet of 1/2 inch plywood, and cut it in half. The floor will be a 4 x 4 piece, and use 2 x 2 wood to make a frame on the inside and along the edges for a nice look."

"Take 6 inch wide PVC piping you can buy from any hardware store, and cut 6 inch pieces off of the PVC, and used them for the legs inside. Use plastic PVC elbow joints to connect them together to a perfect 4 foot square that you could raise and lower pretty easy into the whelping box."

"When you have the plastic PVC piping inside the box, it makes it harder for the mom to lay down against the sides of the box, when she is feeding her puppies, and if one gets stuck behind her when she moves around all the time, it gives the puppy that added air-vent below that keeps the moms weight off the puppy, and the puppy can survive."

13. Are Rawhide Treats Good for Your Irish Setter?

"By all means, give your dog some rawhide treats! They are good for them, and dogs love them! Rawhide is great for cleaning your dog's teeth, and it also gives your Irish Setter something to chew on, besides your couch or favorite pair of shoes!"

"When looking at rawhide, try to find the biggest pieces, because you don't want the smaller bone fragments that break off the smaller ones, for your Irish Setter. You would be smart to ask your vet, or shop around for the best quality rawhide you can find. It comes in many different styles, and even fun filled treats inside some of them, to keep your Irish Setter entertained!"

"It is best to supervise your dog with a rawhide chew, as it could come apart, and get lodged in the dog's throat, but that is extremely rare, but still could happen, just as any toy or treat you give your pet, should be supervised."

"When your dog has chewed on a big piece of rawhide, and it is soft and gooey, take it away, and give them a new one, let the old one harden up again, and you can give it back to them later."

"The good thing about rawhide is it is good for your Irish Setter's stress level. A bored Irish Setter will have more stress, because he or she is bored, and a rawhide treat will keep them more occupied and entertained!"

"It is hard to tell if good rawhide comes from the United States, or other countries, so it is best to get the best quality you can find."

14. How to Stop Your Irish Setter From Eating Their Own Stools

"The last thing you want to do is see your Irish Setter eating his or her own feces stools! You would not want any guests or family members over, and your dog does that in front of them!"

"If your Irish Setter is eating his or her own feces stools, you might want to increase their daily exercise activity, and make sure you are feeding him or her, a high quality dog food."

"There are chewable treats for dogs, which will make even the worst offender stay away from his or her own feces stools, as it goes right thru the intestines of your dog, and out in the stools, with a taste they will hate, but will not harm them!"

"The active ingredient is pretty close to red hot chili peppers, and your dog will hate the taste, but the treats do not harm your dog at all, but they will not eat their feces stools anymore, thereby taking care of the problem."

"This is not to be used in puppies, or dogs that are nursing, or dogs with any medical problems. Ask your vet about dog treats that will stop your Irish Setter from eating his or her own stools, and you could just as easily order it online also if you search for it."

"The last thing you want at a party or family get together is your Irish Setter showing off his bad habits of eating their own feces, it just is not good, and you need to take care of it immediately".

15. Why Your Irish Setter Needs a Good Soft Bed to Sleep In

"You would want to give your new Irish Setter puppy, or any adult Irish Setter dog, a nice big soft bed to sleep in. Irish Setters are very big dogs, and if they sleep on the hard ground, or floor, they get callouses on their body, just like camels do, and it is not good for them."

"Irish Setters have such large bodies, they need a soft place to lie down, and you should make sure they have a comfortable place to sleep."

"Usually a dog that is sleeping on a hard surface, gets calluses on their bodies, and if it gets worse, they called that Hygroma, which can become infected, and filled up, and need medical attention. The best way to avoid this is to give your Irish Setter a nice soft bed, and they are going to be a very big dog, and fun, and you don't want them to be in pain later in life."

"The pet business if filled with tons of different types of soft plush beds for puppies and dogs. Give your Irish Setter the bed he or she deserves, and they will love you for it!"

"It is not uncommon for adult Irish Setter dogs to sleep twice as long as people threw out the day and night. Your Irish Setter spends a lot of time sleeping, and if he or she has any arthritis or joint problems, they even have special orthopedic beds for older dogs."

"Your Irish Setter will appreciate having a nice soft comfortable bed to call his or her own. Just like you enjoy a nice soft mattress to sleep on, your Irish Setter deserves the same from you, and being that they are such a large size breed dog, they need it even more!"

16. How to Stop Your Irish Setter From Running Away or Bolting Out the Door

"It is not good at all for your Irish Setter puppy or dog to try to run away every chance they can, or bolt out the door whenever you open it! This could be one of the worst things for your puppy or dog, as they could be lost or hurt, and you don't want that! The reason they like to run away, is many different reasons, and if you can curb some of the reasons, it will make it much better for you and your puppy or dog."

"Dogs are usually rewarded when they break out and run away, and explore. They can find other dogs they can run with sometimes, or a cat they can chase down the street, or up a tree. They might see a child that they never saw before, and the child might want to pet them. They might find a mate dog out there, and they want to go to them."

"They could tip over the neighbors trash cans, and find interesting things to rummage thru, and just all sorts of reasons a dog gets rewarded when they break out, or bolt out the door, and take off on you, but still so dangerous!"

"Whatever the reason your Irish Setter is trying to break out, if you can contain some of the ways and reasons, it will make it much easier for you. For example, if the fence is loose in a certain spot, and he or she gets out there, by all means fix it!"

"If the dog can see the mail delivery person coming each day, maybe you could put some tarps up so your dog can not see out, or even moving the mail box to a different location, so you dog does not see it anymore, and take away the temptation that gets them wound up in the first place."

"You want to make it less inviting for your puppy or dog to break out, than to stay around and stay home. If you take away some of the obstacles, and make it harder for them to break out, that is good. You also want to make their desire to leave and runaway less too."

"Some dogs just have a natural instinct to want to get away, and be with the pack, be it dogs or humans. It's a natural instinct, and you can curb it, but you can't take it out of your dog."

"You can learn a few home trick remedies, but nothing would be as good as you and your dog attending dog obedience classes together! You would learn much more in detail, and your dog would respect you, and wait for your guidance; it would want to please you, rather than bolting out the door on you."

"Some little tricks you can do yourself, would be to be by the door, and you open the door, when your dog comes, if he or she stops at the door, and does not go out, you give them praise and a treat."

"If he or she bolts from the door, you get them back, and then you do it again. This time, you let the door almost come closed, but you keep it open just a little bit. When the dog sits or stays and the door is still partly open, you give them a treat and praise again. Repeat this until you have the dog sitting in front of the door, and he or she does not go out, and you give them praise and a treat, until you could rely on praise only."

"The only time the dog should want to go thru the open door, is when you go first, and tell the dog to "Come" and he or she will follow you. If you never go out the door or call them, they should stay inside, unless called."

"Any dog that breaks out of his or her yard, or bolts from an open door, can be a tragic situation for the dog, especially if there are passing cars nearby. You want to take care of this problem immediately, before your puppy or dog gets hurt."

17. Some Helpful Tips for Raising Your Irish Setter Puppy

"Before you bring your Irish Setter puppy home, you might want to get things ready for him or her. Some of the things you might want to get would include:"

"Some dog crates, one or two for the house, and one for the car. You would want to get some fencing for the back yard, and as you know, Irish Setter are going to be really big dogs when they grow up! You might as well get the heaviest duty dog gear you can buy, it will be worth it!"

"You would want to get your home and yard ready just like you would for a new baby almost. You would want to puppy proof your home, nothing that would hurt the puppy should be out, and all cabinets should be locked."

"For outside the house, all pools and hot tubs should be fenced in, and all gates should be locked and double checked. A Irish Setter can really put a lot of weight into something, if you think they might get out, they probably can, so make it even tougher, it's a Irish Setter!"

"Collars and leashes, you would actually need several, for training purposes. A short one for training and a long one for walks you go on. You should not leave a collar on a puppy while unsupervised, it could get caught and choke the puppy."

"A collar should be used only when training. They are common on most every dog, just make sure you have a good fitting one, and watch your puppy, to make sure he or she does not get it caught, a collar should not be left on, but dog owners do it all the time it seems, so just be extra careful."

"You should never have to yell or scream, or get carried away when trying to train your Irish Setter. If you feel he or she is not moving forward, take a break, and try it again in a bit. Make sure you are not the one who is trying to hard. To puppy will learn the commands, over time, no puppy gets it all right the first time, there will be mistakes, but in the end, you will have a much better trained dog. One you and your family can live with for many years to come!"

"While your puppy is still young, you should enroll yourself and your new puppy in as many dog obedient classes that you think you could handle. This will be the best experience for both you and your puppy, and you both will bond much better together, and get the most out of it. For the long haul, it is totally worth it!"

"Hopefully your puppy has already seen the vet before you even brought him home, just for a checkup at least. You should at this time, find a reputable vet in your area, and set your new puppy up for regular visits and exams all puppies and dogs need to have on a regular basis."

"The first day you bring you new puppy home, try to make it when you have plenty of time off of work or school, so that the puppy is not immediate left alone, and insecure. It is best to spend plenty of time with the new puppy, especially the first couple of days."

"If you can take a sock or towel with you, and let the mother and any other siblings roll around on it, it would be a good comfort blanket to help your new puppy adjust in his new home."

"Your puppy might whine, whimper and cry the first couple of nights, this is natural really. It will go away eventually, as this is how its mother raises the baby. It whines when it cries for its mother, when it wants to eat, and is crying out for attention."

"That is where the towel or sock with the mothers scent rubbed on it, comes in handy to put inside the crate. You would also want some good solid stainless steel bowls for food and water. You should check with your vet on a proper food and feeding time, usually twice daily, at the same times, but some vets recommend different diets for your Irish Setter, so check with your vet first."

"Teach your new Irish Setter puppy to be a part of the family. Irish Setter dogs like to be included with the family, they are not that happy if just left in the back yard, they like to be included with the family, so keep that in mind and have fun with your new Irish Setter puppy!"

"You can teach your new puppy to go to the bathroom outside. You need to take your new puppy outside several times a day. A puppy cannot tell you when they have to go pee or poop they just go. It is your responsibility to know to take the puppy outside, since they will have to go to the bathroom several times each day."

"When you take your new puppy outside, teach them to eliminate in a certain spot, and then give them a treat and praise. Continue to do this, each time you take them outside, tell them to go "potty" and wait for them to go. As soon as they are done, reward them with praise and a treat, and take them back inside."

"When take your puppy outside to go to the bathroom, when you take him or her out, just stand still, and let the dog do their business. When they are finally doing their business, while they are doing it, just stand there, and say, "Good Potty" "Good Baby" and talk sweet to them, until they are done."

"When they are done, give them praise and a treat. Continue doing this until you only use praise, and the dog will learn to go outside, and do his or her businesses quickly, and then back inside."

"Under no circumstances should you ever leave your new puppy unsupervised. If you have to do something, he or she should be in their crate, safe and sound."

18. HOW TO SOCIALIZE YOUR IRISH SETTER PUPPY

"All dogs should be socialized as puppies, before they are 16 weeks old. This is the most important time in a dog's life. This is the time that will shape them, and determine what kind of friendly dog they will turn out to be."

"This is the time your puppy should get to know people, other dogs and animals. This is the most important part of a puppy's life, and will determine how his or her behavior is when they grow up, and what type of personality they will have."

"This is the most important time to get close and bond to your Irish Setter puppy, and introduce your puppy to things in his or her life. You may introduce your puppy to rides in cars, or meeting new people, or going on a walk in the park."

"Your puppy will also be meeting new surroundings and things on his or her own, like plants, wild animals, birds, cats, things they might come across on their own, without you, so they need to be prepared for life."

"You want your new puppy to adjust well to his or her new world. You don't want to leave them in a kennel all day, which would not be good for them, or you."

"Every single puppy needs to be socialized so they have a good understanding of
their environment, and all the things that
go on around them, no matter where you
obtained your puppy from, all puppies
need to be socialized."

"The time to socialize your puppy is up
to 16 weeks old. You don't want them to
start having problems like separation
anxiety, excessive barking, chewing up
your favorite items, urinating and defecating in the wrong spots."

"If you plan to take your puppy or dog to
obedience training classes, you will have a
much more enjoyable time if your puppy
is already familiar with things. You should

take the time to socialize him or her, so they can have an excellent opportunity of being the best dog you want them to be!"

"You want to socialize your puppy, because when he or she is older, you want them to get along well with humans, other animals, and society in general. You don't want a puppy that hides or is scared of every little thing around him or her."

"You don't want a puppy or dog that barks at every moving thing, or anything else like that. Every single person the dog comes in contact with, will be a sign that the puppy that did not get socialized properly at an early age. Give your puppy the love and respect it deserves, and have fun with him or her also while doing this socializing; your dog will love you for it later!"

"A big reason some of the dogs in the United States have to be euthanized each year is just for the simple fact the dog did not get socialized when he or she was a puppy. And for that sad fact, the puppy or dog just did not have the skills to act appropriately in family, public, or tough situations."

"It's a poor fact, that if most all the dogs had been properly socialized as puppies, they would have been much gentler and well behaved dogs when they are grown up. It's not that hard to socialize your new puppy, and it can be fun and rewarding!"

"You don't really want your do go grow up, where you just leave them in the backyard, and they don't know how to interact with the family, and are a nuisance to the neighborhood in general. One that destroys or digs holes all over your backyard, you have a choice when you get your puppy. You can make him or her responsible, friendly, well behaved, and good natured dog."

"It's nice when you have a dog you can trust, and everyone should be able to trust their dog. You want your dog to be able to make rational decisions when he or she is out and about with you. He should be capable of being around lots of people, without jumping up on all of them, and barking nonstop at them."

"From the day your new Irish Setter puppy is born, the mother has already started the process for you. When she has the litter, she will make sure she licks each one, to stimulate them, and they can urinate and defecate, and the mother will take care of this, it is natural for them to do that."

"As the pups get older, the mother will use smell, sounds, and body language to teach the pups natural skills. This is also the time when the mother might discipline her puppies; don't be alarmed, this is natural also."

"The puppies learn from each other while together in the litter. They play, wrestle, and generally learn to live with each other and get along, and get to know each other."

"When your puppy is roughly 7 to 8 weeks old, this is the crucial time to play with them, with human hands, with human touch and smells. This is also a good time for the breeder or owner to start puppy on household training."

"You do not want your Irish Setter puppy or dog to be afraid of humans when they grow up. It is extremely important to spend some quality time with your puppy, just playing, hugging, and loving him or her. You want them to get used to you, and other members of the household as well."

"Most new puppies arrive at their new home around 8 weeks old or older. When your new puppy arrives, you want to immediately start socializing them with everything around them. You want to also remember not to give them something that will scare them too much, or damage them. You would not want to immediately introduce them to an aggressive dog, which is too aggressive for them, or one that could scar them for life. Just use common sense when dealing with your new puppy."

"If you have a big giant hole in your backyard, you would not want to just let your new puppy go, and find the hole by accident. You would want to introduce your puppy to his new surroundings with a tour, so he or she would feel safe, but still interested and alert."

"It is good to introduce your new Irish Setter puppy to a chew toy at this time. This will be used for training purposes. You should pick up your puppy and give him or her, the love all puppies' desire. Rub their belly, scratch their head, talk to them gently, and your new puppy will love it so much, you will too!"

"Now that your new puppy is home, it is important to start to teach him or her some basic commands right away. They should learn commands like sit, stay, down, etc...."

"This is the time you want to introduce your puppy to lots of new experiences, like loud radios, kids playing and yelling, household appliances that make noises, like vacuum cleaners, televisions, dish-washers, lawn mowers, etc..."

"It's good to let your new puppy discover for him or herself, while you give good supervision. Let them walk around and discover the plants in your yard, the toys in your kid's bedroom, and the tools in the garage. Don't let them get hurt, but let them explore, so they are not afraid of their surroundings."

"If your dog is going to be living in a high rise, or on a boat or yacht, get them used to elevators, or getting on and off the boat safely. Take your puppy out for walks and let them meet other dogs on leashes. Let people stop and pet your dog, you don't want your dog to grow up to be afraid of people, and then bite them out of fear!"

"It is good to introduce your new puppy to as many people as you can, between 8 and 12 weeks old. This is the stage that it is most important to socialize your new Irish Setter puppy with people. Encourage them to be gentle with your puppy, to touch, to play with, to pet, and to give treats, in a non-threatening manner."

"It is not recommended to take your new puppy to off leash dog parks, as some parks have many dogs. Some of the dogs will not have been vaccinated, and it is still your choice, but you would probably not send your kids to school, with other kids that have not been vaccinated, if you knew about it."

"Don't assume all the dogs at the off leash dog park have been socialized properly, and they are all vaccinated, so just use caution around dog parks."

"If you want to teach your puppy or dog to ride in the car with you, take him or her on short trips at first. If you put a new puppy or dog in a car, and take it on a trip across the country, the puppy or dog might never want to get back in the car again!"

"Take short trips, and make the first couple to fun places! If your dog's only ride is to go to the vet, or somewhere else unpleasant, they will associate that ride with unpleasant things, so make it happy for them!"

19. How to Stop Your Irish Setter Dog From Excessive Barking

"If your Irish Setter puppy or dog is barking excessively, it could be from many different things. He or she could be being caught on, or under a fence. He or she could be barking at other dogs in the neighborhood, or they could be lonely and feel depressed."

"Dogs bark for many many reasons really. It would be impractically to think that your puppy or dog would never bark again, because some barking is actually good for a dog, and you!

Dogs bark to alert their owners or danger, or a suspicious person lurking around. But a dog that just barks and barks, and

93

you don't seem to know why, not only bothers you, but it usually always disturbs the neighbors as well."

"One of the first things you need to find out is why your dog is barking in the first place. Does he or she see a squirrel or cat in a tree every day, and bark at that? Or does your puppy or dog not get enough exercise, and is left alone outside for long periods of time, and they are barking from boredom. After you find out why they are barking, it is much easier to correct the problem then."

"Puppies will naturally bark if they are playing and running around, it is in their nature to playful bark that is normal. If you cannot notice what your dog is barking at, sometimes they can see or smell things that you cannot, so you might need to take a closer look again. You should also make sure you have your Irish Setter puppy or dog checked out by a vet, to make sure he or she is fine, before you try to correct the problem."

"It is good to have a nice place for your dog to sleep, like a dog house, a dog bed, and a nice place to make their own. You would not like it, if you had to sleep outside, and no one gave you a house or bed to sleep in, so be good to your dog."

"Here are some ways to help curb your dogs barking. If your dog is barking, and you open the door to let him or her in, you are just reinforcing them to bark, each time they want to come inside. When they bark, they know you will come to the door

and let them in, and the barking is working for them."

"If you go to the door and stand there
and scream at them like a raving lunatic,
they will think you are joining them in the
celebration, and they will want to bark
even more! You are barking to them, so
they want to bark also, and join in!"

"If your Irish Setter puppy or dog it
barking and you come and baby him, and
give him or her treats, that is no good.
They will take that as a sign that barking
is what they need to do, to get more attention from you, so you should never reward this type of barking."

"There are several ways to teach your dog that barking is not rewarded. If you are gone all day, and you are aware that your dog barks excessively while you are gone, he or she most likely thinks that if they keep barking, you will show up. Eventually when you show up, you immediately go to the dog, and the barking might stop then. In your dog's mind, he or she has been barking to bring you home, and it worked, you are home finally."

"To cure this type of barking, when you get home, do not immediately go to your dog. Let the dog know that you are not rewarding him for barking. Do not go to the dog until after he or she has settled down, and then you can go to him or her, after the barking has stopped and does not start again for a bit."

"If our dog barks when the phone rings, or your cell phone goes off, teach them to ignore it. You could do this by having a friend or family member, call your phone repeatedly, and you just sit there and do not answer it. With repetition, your dog will bark less and less, and then get bored with the phone all together."

"One of the easiest things to remember when training your dog is to praise or reward your dog when he or she does something you like, and give a negative response to something you do not like. Over time, your dog thru repetition will learn what is acceptable, and what is not acceptable. He or she will be a much better member of the family, and good for them also!"

"There are several ways you could train your dog not to bark when you leave your home. You would need something loud, like a can of rocks, or marbles inside the can, or a garden hose, and you would use these for the negative suggestions. You would leave your home, and then you quietly come back, and just hide outside somewhere in front."

"When you hear your dog barking, use the hose to just put the nozzle over the fence, and squirt him or her, or throw the can of rocks or marbles in their general direction, careful not to actually hit them. The loud noise will scare them, and they will associate the barking with getting wet, or having loud noises come at them, they will eventually tire of the barking."

"You could also use a treat and the command Quiet or Stop. When your dog is barking, you give the command Quiet and when he or she stops barking, you give them a treat and praise, and eventually you would just give them praise."

"With just about any dog, it will never happen overnight. It takes consistence and patience. Your dog will make great progress, and then fall back sometimes, that is only natural. They will move forward again, with patience and good dog training, you can make your dog an excellent family member."

"Sometimes a dog likes to bark at a mail delivery person, or delivery person that comes around. In your dog's eyes, this person is coming into their territory and is an intruder, an unwelcome guest, and your dog barks continuously at this person. The person usually does leave in a short period of time, and the dog thinks that his barking has made the intruder go away, and he or she has done a good job!"

"If you wanted to cure this type of barking, and you were friends with your mail person or delivery person, you could tell them your training method, and give them a bag of snacks to carry with them. Each time they would come to your house, they could give the dog a snack over the fence, and the dog would come to think of this person as a welcome guest, instead of an intruder, and the barking would settle down after a bit."

"The best way to train any dog is for you and your puppy or dog to enroll in obedience classes together. You will have a much better understanding of just basic dog techniques, and you would bond with your dog even more!"

20. WHEN YOUR IRISH SETTER HAS DOG FOOD OR TOY AGGRESSION TENDENCIES

"If you give your new Irish Setter puppy or dog, a bowl of dog food, and then they growl at you, or try to get between you and the food bowl, they have a dog food aggression. When they have a food aggression, sometimes that carries into toys and playthings also they like to be over protective of."

"When your dog shows this type of aggression, he or she is telling you that they are the alpha male dog, and you are not. You have to change this behavior right away, before it gets out of control."

"Your dog might not even be aware that he or she is doing this. They might see you as the bad person, because you come and always take things away from them. They might consider their food or toy something you want to take from them, and they want to protect it from you."

"Your Irish Setter might think that he might not get any more dog food when what you gave him or her is gone, and they growl at you when you get close, because they don't want you to get it. Each time your dog growls and you back away, it reinforces their bad behavior. They think they are being rewarded by you backing off and leaving them alone, they won the battle in their mind."

"If your Irish Setter is sharing a food bowl with another dog and being aggressive, it is best to simply use two food bowls, and separate the dogs while they eat. If your dog seems like he might bite, it is best to stay back, and then correct the problem by making them work for the food."

"One way you could teach your Irish Setter puppy or dog is, you could put the food bowl down on the ground empty. The dog will look at the empty food bowl, be a little bit confused, and then look up at you. You would be in charge now, you could add some food to the bowl a little at a time, and get down close to your dog, and bond with him or her while they are eating."

"You should get your puppy or dog used to you touching and petting him or her while they are eating. They should get used to human touch, but be very careful, use caution; you want to get your Irish Setter used to you at meal time."

"If your dog is showing you signs of aggression, you could slowly and carefully hand feed your dog. You could use this time to teach him or her "stay" and "sit" commands."

"You could walk by your dog's food bowl, and while he or she is looking, throw in a treat every now and then, your dog will look forward to you coming around their food bowl and leaving treats or snacks sometimes, and you will be an invited guest."

"You could also substitute their food, you simply take the food bowl of food away from them, and then put down something better they would love to eat, and then they get the idea of giving something up, to get something even better from you!"

"You need to be gentle with your puppy or dog; yelling or screaming your lungs out is not going to help the situation. Be persistent, and over time, you can teach your puppy or dog to not be so aggressive at mealtime, or with their favorite toys. It is always a good idea to enroll yourself and your puppy or dog into obedience classes."

21. How to Stop Your Irish Setter Puppy or Dog From Biting

"It is natural when puppies are young, to want to bite on something, especially if they are still teething. A young puppy whose teeth are breaking thru their gum lines, will want something to chew on. They will chew on a person's hand, to help the teething pain go away, just like babies like to chew on teething rings."

"When puppies are playing, they are going to want to snap and bite, but that is because they are playing, and it is completely natural when they do this. The sooner you can teach your puppy or dog not to bite, the better!"

"It is not a very good practice to play tug-a-war or chase your puppy around the house or yard type games. This will only make the matter worse in most cases. The puppy or dog will get all excited or scared, and his natural instincts will take over, and that might include biting or snapping at you."

"You should never smack or hit your puppy, especially in the face. They might end of being afraid of you, or worse, they might think of you as a threat, and then try to bite you!"

"The other reason a puppy or dog might try to bite you, is they are trying to prove their dominance over you. Just like, they are the alpha male dog, and you have to take care of this problem right away, before someone gets bit. If you do not teach your puppy to not bite, he or she will not know, and think it is acceptable behavior. You as the puppy or dog owner, have to put a stop to it right away."

"If your puppy starts to bite your hand or foot, give them the command "No" and then replace your foot or hand with a chew toy. You need to teach them that biting you is unacceptable behavior."

22. WHAT TO EXPECT BEFORE AND DURING YOUR DOG HAVING PUPPIES

"Dogs will usually give birth roughly 63 days after breeding. This is the time you would want to get things ready for the new mother. You would want to build a whelping box, so the mother has a nice safe place to raise the puppies."

"Before the mother gives birth, she will usually start digging, scratching, trying to find a place to hide, to make a place like a den to give birth, as their natural instinct will take over. I have seen a dog in the woods, give birth with not help from a human, and when I got there, she had cleared a spot in the leave, and pushed it all away, and make a small den, and her 5 puppies were doing fine, and all healthy."

"You would not want your dog to have puppies in the woods, but that was a site I witnessed. You would hopefully have a whelping box make up for your dog, that has safely rails inside, so the mother does not squeeze any of the puppies, and she can't lean up against them, and smoother then by accident."

"It is better if you are with the mother, while she is giving birth. You mostly need to be there, in case the cord is wrapped around the puppies head, or the mother cannot get it out herself, after trying. Always let the mother do it herself, if there is a problem, has clean towels, and a sterile pair of scissors handy to cut the umbilical cord in case of emergency."

"Usually the mother will have one puppy at a time, sometimes pretty quick, and sometimes about an hour apart. When each puppy comes out, the mother will take the sac, and lick it and get it open, and then start licking the baby, and this will get the puppy to breath. Next, the mother will chew part of the umbilical cord off, with a long piece still hanging on the babies, they she will chew off even more later."

"Your dog will appreciate you more, by being with her, and be gentle with her, and tell her she is doing well. If for any reason something goes wrong, you would need to make sure you get the sac off the puppy, and then take the towel to dry them up quickly, and then rub their chest to try to get some air into them, so they can breathe. You would then take the sterile scissor, and cut the umbilical cord, and then give the puppy to the mother so she can lick her, then put her on one of the teats so the baby can immediately eat."

"Depending on how your dog is, and how she feels most comfortable, some dogs will squat and give birth, others will lay on their side, and let them come out that way. Giving birth is a natural thing, you should just be present for emergencies, and to sooth your dog."

"A dog out in the wild that has her puppies on her own, will be much more protective of her pups, and maybe even growl or bite you if you try to get close to the puppies. If you are right there in the box with her, when she is giving birth, and you are helping her, and putting each puppy on a teat, and making sure they all get milk, she will much more likely welcome you into her pack, and it will be much easier for you, when it comes time to socialize the puppies."

"At roughly 2 weeks, the puppies eyes and ears will be opening, and then not much longer after that, the puppies will be playing with each other, and jumping around, and nursing from mom nonstop almost it seems. You should have your dog checked out by a vet, before birth, and after birth, and you can take the puppies in also for a checkup."

"Mothers will usually start to wean their puppies about 5 weeks of age. You will start your puppies on a feeding schedule, and its' best to search for the proper amount and schedule online, but a little common sense can go a long way. All puppies need to be vaccinated against puppy diseases at the proper time. You can have your vet do this, and some pet stores offer this service, and sometimes you can administer the shots yourself, but learn before you do that."

"All dogs must have a rabies shot, and only a qualified vet can administer rabies shots, and not until the puppy has reached 4 months old, and not any sooner than that. The rabies shot is very important, as is the shots that are typically called either 5 in 1, or 7 in 1, and you would give them in a series, after waiting a certain amount of time, you would give another shot, usually 3 sets of shots, but with anything, you should consult your veterinarian, and make sure you read any directions very carefully, before trying to do it yourself."

"I personally have been buying my own shots for years. I usually get them in a box of 25, that I keep chilled, and I buy them on the internet, and they come in a box with dry ice usually, from a well-respected company, one of the biggest I believe, and I do see how it has become harder to buy online, and some companies have discontinued selling to the public, so please do some research."

"While your dog is pregnant, she will require more food and water, she is eating for several now! When the puppies are born, and right after, your mother is going to be hungry. I suggest you give her some canned dog food, that is easy for her to digest, and lay off the dry bits for a bit, make sure she has plenty of water, and the softer food will be more gentle on her system, she since just gave birth. I find the mothers are extremely hungry after giving birth, just something I notice with raising dogs for over 25 years now."

"For the first several weeks, the mother will use her tongue, to stimulate the puppies, and give them bowl movements, and the mother will clean and lick up all the accidents the little puppies make, until they get to much for the mother, usually right around the time she starts weaning them, and you will start feeding them."

"Besides keeping everything clean, your job is not that hard for the first 5 weeks, the mother will be the one doing all the work, as you start to feed the puppies, and clean up the box, you will get much more involved, trust me, I've been cleaning up after dogs and puppies for many years, that's one reason you teach your dog to go in a certain spot, right from the beginning."

"Your dog should already have a regular vet, and he or she should be aware that your dog will be giving birth. If you suspect any unusual activity, or smelly, foul, orange or reddish discharge, or any other thing you might think is wrong, get her to the vet as soon as you can, don't let your dog go thru any pain, and don't let any of the puppies get hurt, if you can help it."

"If you use common sense, and read several different articles about dogs giving birth, that is the best way to teach yourself about it, don't read one article, read several different opinions, you will learn much more that way."

23. What the Benefits of Micro-chipping Your Dog Are to You

"If you've been wondering if micro-chipping your dog is a good thing, it is, if you ask me. It's just like anything, if you ask 7 different veterinarian's the same question, you might get some totally different answers and opinions, so just use your common sense."

"A microchip that is placed inside your dog, usually between the shoulder blades, and with a syringe that looks pretty much like the one dogs get their shots with. The microchip is about the size of a grain of rice. It is inserted by your veterinarian, and different vets sell different packages, but relatively all the same."

"It is really no more painful to your dog then them getting vaccinated, and if you ever lose your dog, this is one of the best ways of hoping to get him or her back."

"The microchip is basically a transmitter, that the skin just grows right back over, and it stays with your dog, for their entire life. The transmitter does not require any batteries or maintenance. It is embedded with a number the company supplies and your veterinarian will have much more details on, you will have to pay a onetime fee for this service."

"When a scanner that a vet or animal shelter should have on hand these days, maybe some smaller out in the country vets still don't have access to one, but if they do, the scanner would make the transmitter give us a signal, that the scanner could read. Since it is universal, injecting the microchip behind the shoulder blades, but over time and years, some dogs may have growth movement."

"Millions of dogs get lost every year. One of the best ways to make sure your puppy or dog does not get lost in the first place, is to be a responsible pet owner, and make sure your home and yard are puppy and dog proof, just like you might do for a real baby in your home."

"Make sure fences and gates are secure, make sure there are no holes being dug you don't know about. Make sure your dog gets plenty of exercise and care and love, so they don't feel the need to go elsewhere."

"If for some reason your dog becomes lost, the collar and tags might get lost or removed, and then it is nearly impossible to find the rightful owner sometimes, and the worst you can imagine might happen, and with the microchip, it is not a for sure bet, but your odds are much higher of getting your lost dog back, then if you did not have it."

"Hopefully your puppy or dog has a very nice place to live, either indoors or outdoors, and they like their surroundings, and never dream of running or getting away, but if for some reason, they are in heat, or they hear kids playing, or the mail delivery person coming, and they want to escape, or they just get loose by accident, like a small child leaving the door open, and then they are long gone, that microchip is going to play a much bigger role in finding him or her, and I really hope it works for everyone!"

24. How to Get Something Out of a Puppy or Dog's Belly Without Surgery

"If your puppy or dog has chewed up something, and you don't know what to do, you could try this method maybe, but you should always go to or call your veterinarian first, and let them know what you are going to do."

"Now I would not recommend this procedure to anyone really, I just wanted you to know, that there is another option out there, before resorting to costly surgery, that could hurt or kill the puppy or dog, and for those that do not have the money for surgery, I would not want you to leave something dangerous in your puppy or dog."

"If your dog eats some Christmas tree ornaments, the glass kind, or some metal objects, like small staples, pins, or glass fragments, or anything else that is totally dangerous, there is one other way to get the items out, without surgery."

"You would use cotton balls to do this with. You would want to buy some cotton balls, and make sure it is cotton balls, not something on the bag that says cosmetics, as that will have some other type of fibers in it, that would not be good for your dog, so make sure you get the ones that say Cotton Balls."

"For small size dogs, you would use roughly 2 cotton balls, for medium size dogs, you would use about 3 to 5, and for large size dogs, you can use 6 or more.

You would want to cut the cotton balls into smaller sizes. If your puppy or dog swallows glass shreds, from things like Christmas tree ornaments, or other items, you would dip the cotton balls in milk or water, and then the puppy or dog will actually eat it and swallow it. If for some reason your dog does not want to, you can actually force the cotton balls into their throat, and make them swallow it."

"As the cotton works its way through the digestion system, it will pick up all the fragments of glass, even the tiniest of one, and it will get caught in the cotton material, and the cotton will protect the inside linings, so your dog will stay protected. When the puppy or dog defecates, you would want to make sure there is no bleeding, and if there is, take your puppy or dog to the veterinarian immediately."

"If you suspect your puppy or dog of swallowing something, you should take them to the vet. If you think you can do it yourself, you could try this method, as the cotton balls are supposed to entangle all the bad stuff, and protect it when it is coming out the dog's body, and then if everything goes well, you have maybe just saved your dog's life. Even if you take your dog to the vet, you could mention this procedure to your vet, as not every vet is up on everything, and no to veterinarians are the same."

25. How Invisible Fencing Typically Works to Train and Protect Your Dog

"Hopefully this will give you a basic understanding on how invisible fencing for your dog should work, and if it is for you, or not for you, only you can decide if you agree with invisible fencing. Not all yards are the same, and by no means, not all dogs are the same, but it should work for most people that use it correctly."

"The system would usually entail you trenching a trench, or digging up the ground along the path you want your invisible fencing to go. Just pretend it is an invisible wall, and where you put the wires, will be where the invisible fencing will be located at."

"You would want to check with your local utilities or power company before digging up and installing the wires. But it is not that difficult, for the average person, as long as they follow the instructions carefully for the system they purchase."

"Your dog would be fitted with a collar, which has some sensors that stick out, and contact the dog's skin. From what I hear, the dog does not get a shock, but a surprising jolt, and since dogs cannot talk. We will really never know what they feel, until we find a dog that can talk, and we put him or her on television, and they tell us everything that is wrong with dogs, and kids would love that story, but you get the idea!"

"The way it works is, you bury the wires underneath the lawn, so you don't have wire everywhere, or you can also run it along wooden fences, not metal ones, and that could be a boundary wall, so they don't dig out, but you don't have to dig up that section, because a fence is already there, basically making them stop digging out, or jumping up on the fence anymore."

"The collar would require batteries, and a test period, and training sessions with your dog, so that he or she understands what is desired of them, and they are training properly about where they can, and where they cannot go in the yard. They do have systems for inside the home, for dogs that jump over gates, and you could find that on the internet for in-side places."

"You would place red flags along the path of the invisible fencing, for training purposes with your dog. Your dog needs to be able to see the invisible lines first, and that is what the flags are put in the ground for. A system that is working fine, would give the dog several peeps warning him or her that they are getting to close to the fence."

"If they do not move back, they will get a shock or surprise jolt, depending on how you look at it, since the dog can't tell us, and the part you really need to teach your dog, before you let him or her loose or on their own, is to turn away from the fence, and go back."

"You could teach them this, by turning it into a fun game for both of you. You would train your dog, by taking them up to the fence, and when the warning beeping starts to go off, you could turn around and run, and call your dog to come too, and then when he or she comes, you could give them some praise, and teach them to turn back, not go thru it."

"Like anything, you would actually need to teach them to go thru it, so they know what they are in for. Walk with them, and when the warning beeping is going off, let them experience the effect of the surprise, as I'm hoping they are getting a surprise rather than a shock, but if this saves them from running out in the street and getting hit and killed by a car or truck, or getting lose and biting someone, then I believe they need to learn what happens if they don't come back, while you are there, rather than while you are away."

"You would leave the red flags up, until you think your dog is ready for them to be taken down. As with anything you love, take good care of your dog, and watch them and keep an eye on them. If you just use common sense, and follow the directions on the kit you buy, and don't take any short cuts, do it right the first time, it will work, just plan everything ahead of time, and give your dog plenty of time to learn the new system with you, and you both should be happier and safer!"

26. How to Make Sure Your Dog is Eating A Healthy Amount of Food

"You as the dog owner has the responsibility to make sure your dog is not under fed, or over fed. Some mature dogs can have free food out all day long, and eat just the right amount on their own, and some other dogs just might eat nonstop, and hurt themselves, and then you usually have to stop that, and feed them a measured amount twice a day, so they don't over eat, every dog is different."

"Younger puppies and dogs usually are very energetic, and burns off some steam, but you should still exercise them, and take them to obedience classes if you can. Older dogs get more set in their ways, and tend to sleep more as they get older. Older dogs still need exercise, but not long periods of it, it is best to give them plenty of times to go out and exercise with you, just shorter periods of time."

"You can ask your vet what is a best food to give your dog; each vet will have his or her own opinion, and then try to stick with what they tell you. You can also go online and use a weight chart, and determine roughly how much your dog should be eating daily. You can measure that amount into their bowl twice daily, and if they are eating it all, you can increase the amount, to control weight gain or lose, just like decreasing the amount you give them. Your vet should be able to tell you what your dog's daily intake should be, and then try to stick to that."

"Make sure you have plenty of fresh drinking water available at all times for your puppy or dog. If you leave your dog inside a crate, make sure there is amble water supply. Dogs, just like humans, would prefer a nice cool drink of refreshing water, rather than a drink from old warm water, with dog hairs floating in it, gives your dog fresh water as often as you can."

27. Make it Easier and Healthier for Feeding Your Irish Setter

"You can make is much easier on your Irish Setter when it comes to eating. Some dogs you can leave their food out for them, and they do not over eat. Other dogs may over eat until they get bloat, or they gobble it down super-fast, and have gas problems and more serious problems."

"To find out how much your dog should be eating, you should check with your vet. You could also measure your dog's food, and then feed him or her twice a day. If they eat the whole bowl, give them more next time, if they do not eat it all, give them less each time. You could measure it, and then come up with the right amount for your dog for each meal."

"For dogs that gobble down their food so fast, the pet supply places, sell dog bowls that have inserts in the bowl, so the dog would have to slow down to eat. You would never want to give your dog just one meal a day. You should feed them twice a day, and at the same time each day, so they can count on their schedule, just like people seem to love, breakfast, lunch and dinner!"

"For large size dogs, it is harder on them and their joints when they have to bend over, to get their head down to the ground, to get a drink of water, and that is bad for their joints, especially if they are young still. Some pet supply stores sell water and food bowls, that go in a stand and make it higher off the ground, and that makes it easier for your puppy or dog to swallow, as their body is more parallel to the ground while eating."

"A raised water and eating bowl, will make your dog more comfortable when eating, and it's especially great if they have muscle or joint problems, and you won't your dog to have a happy and healthy life."

"Just like people, so dogs don't drink enough water sometimes. If you can get your dog to drink more water, it will be much better and healthier for them. You can get one of the bowls from the pet supply store, that gives a continuous supply of cool water, and your dog might enjoy it even more!"

28. How to Clean and Groom your Irish Setter

"It is very important to clean and groom your puppy or dog on a regular basis to keep them clean and sharp looking, and just nice to smell!"

"When bathing your puppy or dog, make it a fun experience for them each time, and the early your start doing it, the better. This is the time you can inspect your dog completely, so that you can notice any new cuts, scrapes, and rashes, anything that you might not notice when just playing with your dog."

"This is also the perfect time to inspect your puppy or dog's nails, check to see if they are too long, and need to be trimmed. Use cotton balls when cleaning the inside of the ears, never use cotton swabs, as you could damage their ears. Check inside of ears for any foul orders, a sure sign that you need a visit to your local vet. If your puppy or dog shakes his or her head a lot, and try's to scratch at it on a regular basis, your dog could have ear mites, or an infection."

"If you do not wash, comb or brush your dog on a regular basis, they could end with mats in their hair, and those are harder to get out. When matts get wet, they are harder to deal with, so you should try to get them out before the bath."

"Fleas can BA another big problem. Make sure you use good quality flea shampoo, and for serious problems, consult your vet at once. Your veterinarian or pet supply warehouse will also carry some more expensive solutions, that do work very well, that you can usually place on the dog once a month, to cure this problem."

"In order to keep water out of your dog's ears while giving him or her a batch, you could put cotton balls just inside the ear canal, so that water does not get inside the ears, and cause a bacterial infection later."

"After you get the bath ready for your puppy or dog, you do not want to get water in their eyes or ears, and you certainly do not want to put your dog's head underneath the water, unless you want your dog to panic and freak out, not a good idea at all."

"Wet your puppy or dogs hair from the head down, and then apply a good quality shampoo, then lather the dog up, rinse and repeat. During the bath, it is good to talk to your dog, and tell them they are doing a good job, and they will relax more, when they hear the gentleness of your voice."

"After you take your dog out of the bath, you do not want to just let him or her go outside, because they will go directly to some dirt, and roll in it, and all your work will be wasted. You should towel dry them as much as you can, and then let them air dry in a warm place, until they care completely dry, combing or brushing them until they are nice. If you do decide to use a blow dryer on your dog, make sure you set it on the lowest setting, so you don't hurt your dog."

"If your dog gets so dirty, or has more matts than you know what to do with, it is best to go to a professional groomer, and let their experience work for you, and you might just learn a few tricks for next time, when you do it yourself."

29. How to Trim a Puppy or Dogs Nails Properly

"The first thing you should know about dogs nails, is that the blood vessels go down to their nails, and if you cut it to short, it will bleed or hurt the dog. The part you DO NOT want to cut is called the "quick". That part has the pink color to it in white or clear nails. For Dogs with dark nails, it is much harder to see, and you need to be more careful."

"It would pay to get a quality pair of nail clippers, if you are not sure, you can ask your vet, and you could even have them or your groomer, give you a lesson on how to trim the nails yourself. It is not that hard, you just need to be extra careful not to hurt the puppy or dog."

"You would be much better off if you teach your dog when they are a puppy, to have their nails clipped. If your dog is walking around, and you can hear their nails clicking on the floor, it is time to cut them. Some dogs need their nails cut once or twice a month, other dogs can go longer between pedicures."

"Make sure the nail clippers you are using are sharp. You would start at the tip of the nail, and then clip a little bit at a time. When you get close to the quick or pink part, you do not want to cut that. If you do cut that, and it starts to bleed, use a styptic stick or styptic powder, or even baby powder, and apply pressure, until the bleeding stops."

"On dark or black nails, it is very difficult to see the pink sometimes, so you want to do just a little at a time. You can use a nail file to file down the rest, and to file off any sharp edges from clipping."

"This is also the perfect time to inspect your puppy or dogs feet. Some dogs that play outside can get the little burs from the plants outside, and the little prickly thing is stuck in their feet, just like a thorn, and can be infected. I know this from experience, as we had those weeds on our land, and our dog got the smallest one in her foot, and it got infected, and the vet gave us antibiotics until the infection was cured, and then I made sure I removed those kinds of weeds from our property."

"If your puppy or dog did not have his or her dewclaws removed, then it would need to be clipped also. It could be caught up on something when your dog is jumping around. It is the nail on the inside of the front legs, which is a little bit up from the paws, it does not get used, so it might be sharp. Do that one the same way you clip the other nails."

"If you don't trim your dog's nails on a regular basis, the quick will start to get longer over time, the part with the blood vessels. Your dog's nails need to be clipped or filed down, if you can hear them click on the floor when they walk. The dog should be walking on his or her paws, and the nails should not be touching the floor."

"If your dog's nails are too long, it can make it hard for them to walk around properly. It is good to have your dog lay all the way down on the floor while you trim the nails. When you are done trimming your dog's nails, you should give praise and a treat to your dog, because you are going to have to do it again sometime, and you want your dog to cooperate each time."

Vince Stead has been raising dogs since 1985 (over 25 years) and served in the Navy for 8 years. He has worked for himself for the last 20 years, and loves to write books."

OTHER BOOKS BY VINCE STEAD

Sammy the Runaway Mastiff
ISBN# 1-59824-314-4

The Back Yard Kids Club
ISBN# 978-1456406219

How to Get Even and Revenge with Pranks on
Anyone
ISBN# 978-1-45387-727-2

How to Raise your Mastiff Puppy with Good
Behavior
ISBN# 978-1456558802

Vince Stead's 110 Jobs Almost Any Teenager Can
Start
978-1-59824-479-3

Navy Fun
ISBN# 978-1-59824-514-1

Navy Sea Stories
ISBN# 978-1456558666

How to Start Over 101 Self-Employment
Businesses
ISBN# 1-59824-292-X

1 Hope Cottage
New Rd,
Childer Thornton
E85 6 5PY

Louise.
17, Alwyn Gdns
Upton
Chester
CH2 1L

Rhys

Printed in Great Britain
by Amazon.co.uk, Ltd.,
Marston Gate.